4.4/ .5p
COMMUNITY LIBRARY
P9-DVH-641

In the Trees, Honey Bees

By Lori Mortensen
Illustrated by Cris Arbo

Dawn Publications

Dedications

To Martin, Allen, Steven, and Jaimie for their love and support, and my father-in-law, Eugene, who knew honey bees best. — LM

To my Joe. — CA

For the wellbeing of our winged friends, the honey bees, pollinators extraordinare. — The Publisher.

Library of Congress Cataloging-in-Publication Data

Mortensen, Lori, 1955-

In the trees, honey bees! / by Lori Mortensen ; illustrated by Cris Arbo. -- 1st ed.

p. cm.

"This introduction to a wild colony of honey bees offers close-up views of the queen, the cells, even bee eggs, and an understanding of their lives" - Provided by the publisher.

ISBN 978-1-58469-114-3 (hardback) -- ISBN 978-1-58469-115-0 (pbk.) 1. Honeybee--Juvenile literature. 2. Bee culture--venile literature. I. Arbo, Cris, ill. II. Title.

SF523.5.M68 2009

595.79'9--dc22

2008038513

Manufactured by Regent Publishing Services, Hong Kong

Printed July 2010 in ShenZhen, Guangdong, China

10 9 8 7 6 5 4 3

First Edition

Book design and computer production by Patty Arnold, Menagerie Design and Publishing.

Dawn Publications

12402 Bitney Springs Road

Nevada City, CA 95959

530-274-7775

nature@dawnpub.com

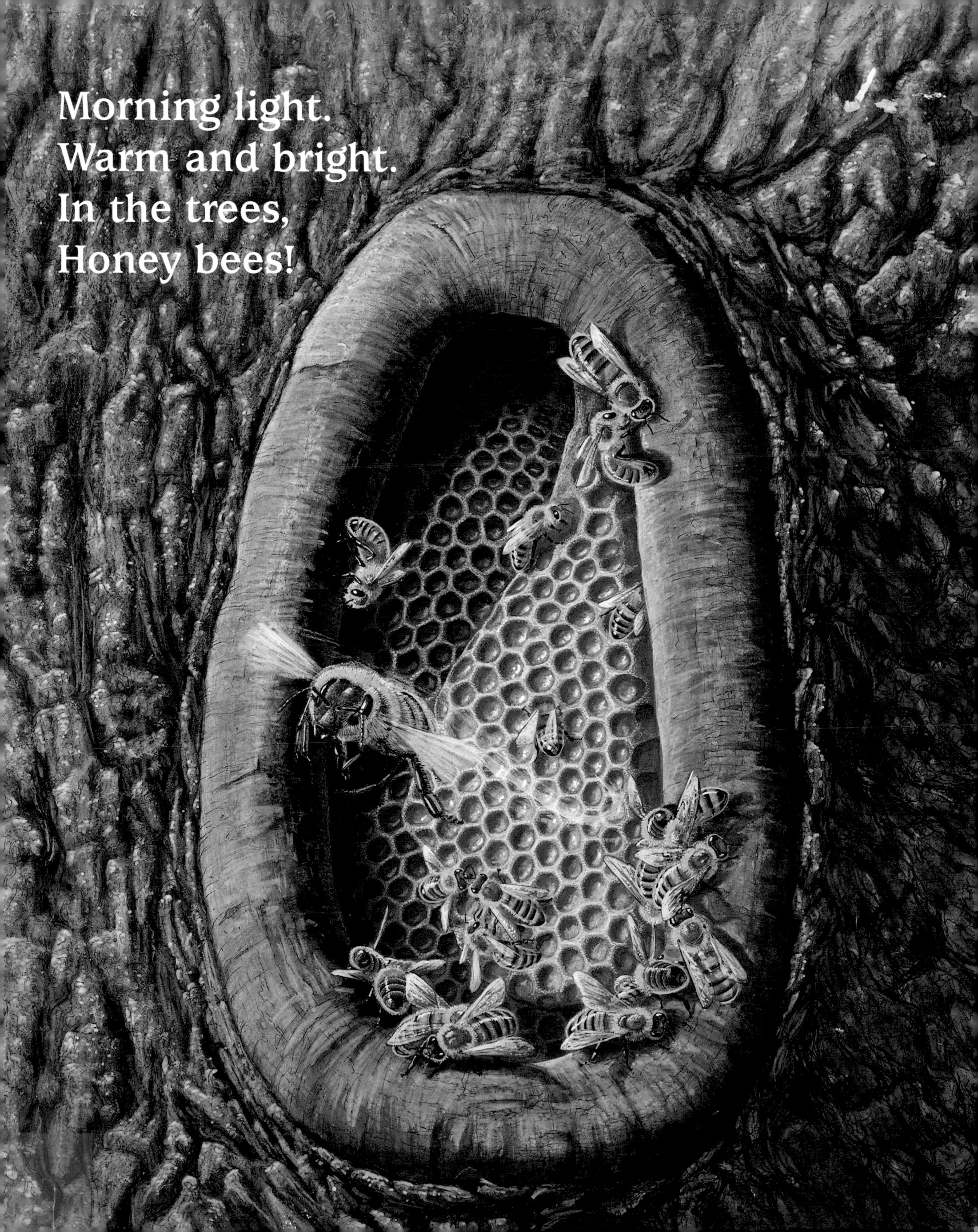

Morning light.
Warm and bright.
In the trees,
Honey bees!

Blossoms out.

Dancing scout.

Many wild honey bees live in hollow tree trunks. When sun warms the air, honey bees search for flowers in bloom. After a scout finds flowers rich with nectar and pollen, it returns to the hive and tells the others where to find them by doing a waggle dance.

Sisters fly
through the sky.

Soon thousands of honey bees leave the hive to find the blossoms. These honey bees are called "worker" bees. They are all sisters.

Nectar sweet.
Pollen treat.

Worker bees collect nectar and pollen to feed the colony. As they fly from blossom to blossom, the bees drink the sweet nectar and collect powdery pollen on their legs.

Harvest home.
Honeycomb.

When the bees are loaded with nectar and pollen, they fly back to the hive. There other worker bees receive the nectar and pollen and store them in wax honeycomb cells.

Feed and clean,
precious queen.

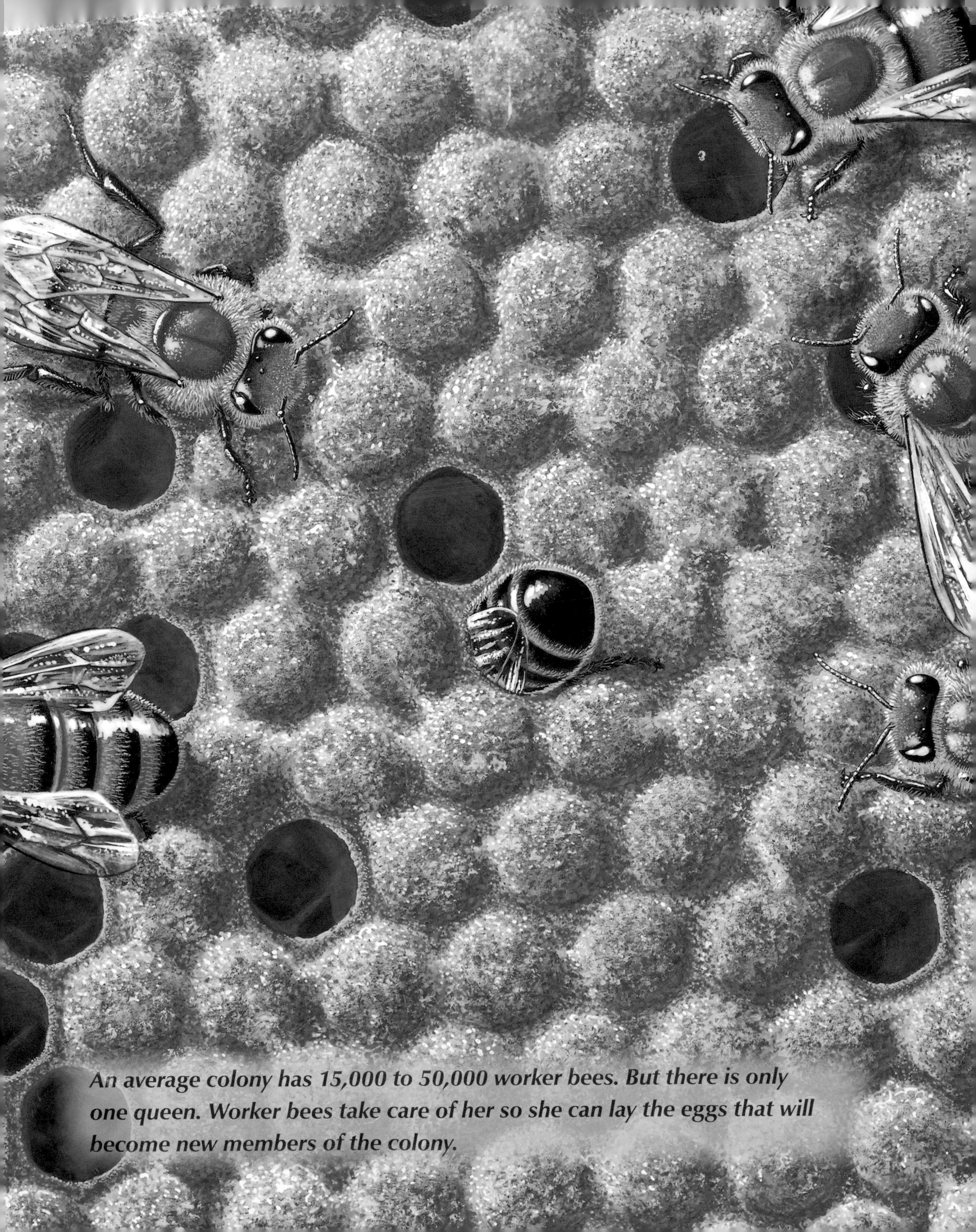

An average colony has 15,000 to 50,000 worker bees. But there is only one queen. Worker bees take care of her so she can lay the eggs that will become new members of the colony.

Lots of food.
Hungry brood.

Three days after the queen lays an egg it hatches into a hungry larva. Nurse bees feed it a rich supply of food from glands in their heads. During its larva stage, nurse bees will feed it more than 100,000 times.

Water drips.
Sip, sip, sip.
Too much heat!
Thousands beat.

Honey bees collect water, too. When temperatures climb, thousands of bees fan their wings. The evaporating water cools the hive.

Bear attack!

Sting and smack.

Guard bees protect the colony. When an intruder tries to get in, the guard bees drive it away and sting. Wasps, moths, skunks and bears are just a few of their enemies.

Shape the wax.
Seal the cracks.

Honey bees build their combs out of wax. Young worker bees secrete wax flakes from special glands under their bodies. They use their mouths and front legs to shape the soft wax into honeycomb.

Honey bees also gather sticky sap from trees. They use it to coat the inside of the hollow tree and seal holes and cracks. It is called "bee glue" or "propolis".

Gather more.
Winter store.

To prepare for the cold months of winter, honey bees make as much honey as they can during spring and summer.

A colony will need about 30 to 60 pounds of honey to survive the winter when the blossoms are gone.

Fading light.
Homing flight.

As the sun sets, the air cools and the blossoms close. Workers fly back to their hive for food, warmth, and shelter with the rest of the colony.

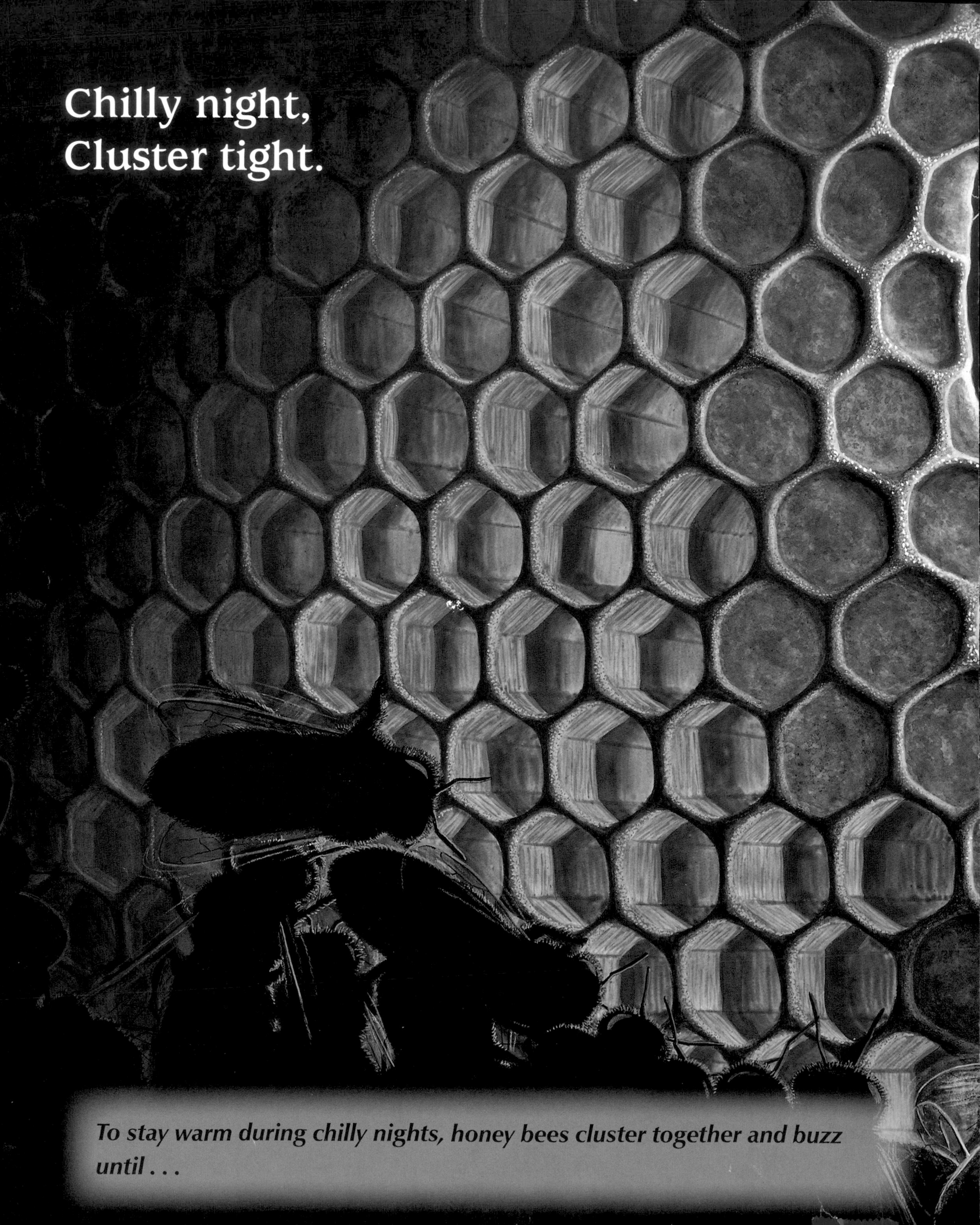

Chilly night,
Cluster tight.

To stay warm during chilly nights, honey bees cluster together and buzz until . . .

Morning light.
Warm and bright.

In the trees,
Honey bees!
Bzzzzzzzzzzzzzzz.

The Buzz About Honey Bees

Have you ever watched honey bees as they buzz from flower to flower? I used to stare at their glistening wings and wonder why they worked so hard. Now I know that each honey bee is a member of a busy colony, doing its part for the hive.

There are over 25,000 species of bees. But only nine species of bees make honey. The most familiar honey bee in the United States is *Apis mellifera*, the European honey bee, introduced by Spanish and English settlers in the 1600s.

Honey bees usually make combs in cavities located in trees, caves, rocks, and boxes that people provide for them. A colony may have up to 50,000 bees and is largest during spring and summer when the hive needs many bees to gather nectar and pollen.

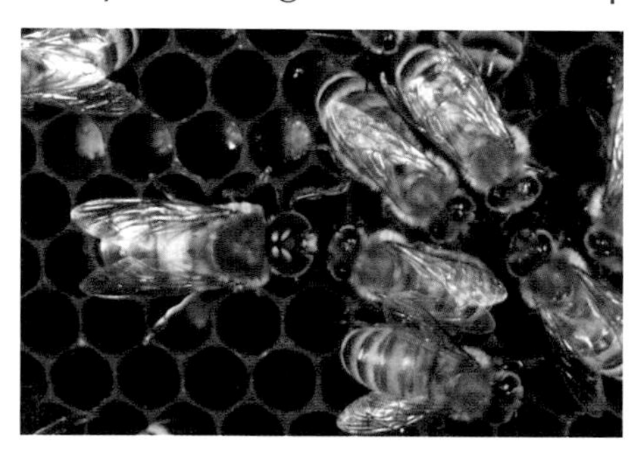

Drone bees are larger than worker bees.
Photo courtesy of MT Frazier, PA State Univ. Dept. of Entomology

There are three types of honey bees—workers, drones, and queens. The workers are females; the drones are males. Although there are thousands of workers, there are only several hundred drones. Their only purpose is to mate with a new queen during her mating flight. After mating, the drones die.

The largest bee in the hive is the queen. She lays up to 2,000 eggs a day. While she lays eggs, workers feed her, groom her, and remove her wastes.

A worker bee's life begins when the queen deposits a tiny, rice-shaped egg in a honeycomb cell. Three days later, a larva hatches. Workers feed it *worker jelly*, and it grows until its body fills the cell. On the ninth day, nursery workers seal the cell with wax. Inside, the larva changes and is now called a *pupa*. About ten days later a new fully-grown adult chews through the wax and joins the colony, ready to work.

There is only one queen bee in a hive. She lays the eggs that develop into new bees.
Photo courtesy of Kathy Keatley Garvey, UC Davis Dept. of Entomology

Although most people see honey bees while they're gathering pollen and nectar, worker bees perform different chores as their bodies mature. They begin in the nursery by cleaning cells, feeding larvae, and caring for the queen.

Next, workers become undertakers by removing dead bodies from the hive. If an intruder dies inside that's too big to remove, such as a mouse, the workers cover the corpse with *propolis*, or "bee glue." The substance acts like plastic bag, sealing bacteria off from the rest of the hive.

When workers are about two weeks old, they collect the nectar and pollen from workers returning from the fields. The workers suck the nectar from the field bee's "honey" stomach and "chew" it, adding important enzymes. After the nectar and pollen are stored in cells, workers fan their wings to remove moisture. When the nectar thickens into honey, workers cap the honey cells with wax.

When worker bees are two to three weeks old they're able to produce wax from glands under their abdomen. Workers use the wax to build the honeycomb cells. An average hive will have 100,000 cells. The colony needs thousands of cells to raise new bees and store honey for winter.

A worker bee's next task is to guard the colony. As bees approach the hive, guard bees check their scent to make sure they're members of the colony. If the hive comes under attack, the guard bees alert other bees to defend the hive.

At about three weeks old, workers fly from the hive as the familiar field bee—its final service to the colony. Field bees forage for blossoms up to three miles away.

A field bee visits 50 to 100 flowers on each trip and makes about ten trips a day. At each flower, the field bee drinks nectar and gets dusted with pollen. It packs the pollen into special "baskets" on its back legs. Field bees visit two million flowers to make one pound of honey. An average colony can make about two pounds of honey a day when the flow of nectar is strong.

Honey bees aren't the only ones who like honey. People have been harvesting honey since prehistoric times. Previously, people often destroyed the colony to get the honey. When people began harvesting the honey, while preserving the colony, they became *beekeepers*. Early beekeepers made hives out of mud, hollow logs, and coiled straw baskets. Today, hives are made from wooden boxes. Inside are frames with comb that can be removed, the honey taken out, and then replaced. In a good season, the beekeeper may harvest between 100 and 150 pounds of honey per hive. The beekeeper leaves plenty for the colony too—their food for the winter.

Together, beekeepers and field bees perform another vital function—*pollination*. As field bees buzz from flower to flower, they transfer pollen from plant to plant enabling the plant to bear fruit. Today, about one-third of everything we eat depends on pollination by honey bees.

Although people have tended honey bees for thousands of years, honey bees are still wild. A colony may leave the beekeeper's hive and find a new home in a hollow tree. Maybe one day you'll see a honey bee flying from flower to flower. When you do, you won't need to wonder where it's going or what it's doing. You'll know it's a member of a busy colony doing its part for the hive.

How to Learn More about Honey Bees

Heiligman, Deborah, *Jump Into Science: Honeybees*, National Geographic Books, 2007.

Kalman, Bobbie, *The Life Cycle of a Honeybee*, Crabtree Publishing Company, 2006.

Watch "Tales from the Hive" by NOVA or see the NOVA Online website which has excellent photos, transcripts and links: www.pbs.org/wgbh/nova/bees/

The National Honey Board has a fact-filled website at www.honey.com/consumers/kids/beefacts.asp, including teacher guides.

At www.gobeekeeping.com there is a free coloring book about bees, short biographies of the "giants" of beekeeping, and advice for those interested in becoming amateur beekeepers.

Children's author Lori Mortensen has always liked honey bees—she just wasn't sure they liked her. If a honey bee flew around her head when she was a child, she jumped up and ran away. Today, Lori thinks honey bees are great. They're one of the fascinating subjects she writes about while she lives with her family in the foothills of Northern California. When she's not watching honey bees in her garden, or enjoying visits from wild turkeys, red-tailed hawks and Canadian geese, she's at her keyboard working on her latest fiction or nonfiction project. To learn more about Lori and her books, visit her website at www.lorimortensen.com.

Cris Arbo used a wild hive in her own backyard in Buckingham, Virginia, as the model for this book. In her imagination she climbed right inside the hive to offer a bee's-eye view of the world. Cris received her degree in art and theater from William Paterson University. Her art has appeared in books, magazines, calendars, cards, murals, and in animated feature films, TV shows, and commercials. When not at the drawing board she gardens and explores the beautiful countryside near her home. She and her husband, author Joseph Patrick Anthony, are frequent speakers at schools and conventions. This is the fourth book she has illustrated for Dawn Publications.

SOME OTHER BUGGY BOOKS FROM DAWN PUBLICATIONS

Eliza and the Dragonfly by Susie Rinehart, illustrated by Anisa Claire Hovemann, is a charming story revolving around the beauty and wonder of the hidden world that can be found in a local pond.

The Web at Dragonfly Pond by Brian "Fox" Ellis, illustrated by Michael S. Maydak—a real-life story of fishing with father that reveals how nature's food chain is connected.

Under One Rock: Bugs, Slugs and Other Ughs by Anthony Fredericks, illustrated by Jennifer DiRubbio. No child will be able to resist looking under a rock after reading this rhythmic, engaging story.

On One Flower: Butterflies, Ticks and a Few More Icks by Anthony Fredericks, illustrated by Jennifer DiRubbio. A goldenrod flower is a minibeast park: a whole community of interesting animals. Watch out for the ambushbug!

My Monarch Journal by Connie Muther, photographs by Anita Bibeau, is the record of a miracle: stunning close-up photographs of metamorphosis, questions for students, room for notes, and an explanation of what is happening.

Dawn Publications is dedicated to inspiring in children a deeper understanding and appreciation for all life on Earth. To view our titles or to order, please visit us at www.dawnpub.com, or call 800-545-7475.